BEAUTIFUL SCARS:

ELEGIAC BEAT POEMS
(2ND EDITION)
BY

EDWARD VIDAURRE

El Zarape Press

McAllen, Texas

Published by El Zarape Press: McAllen, Texas.

Vidaurre, Edward.
Beautiful scars: elegiac beat poems/by Edward Vidaurre.
ISBN—13: 978-1-7328106-1-7
1. Beat—Poetry. 2. Elegiac—Poetry. 3. Love—Poetry. 4. American poetry--Latino American authors. I. Title. 2nd Edition

Cover Art Photograph by Edward Vidaurre
Published by El Zarape Press: McAllen TX USA

Printed in the United States of America.

DEDICATION

To Bob Kaufman's silence

This book is for my family: the two girls that hold my heart by a string on a daily basis, Lilly and Bella.

In memory to those gone too soon:

To my "Pop," Eloy, The Lion--Eloy Alonzo Romero, to my father-in-law Reynaldo Ramírez Esparza Jr., to my biological dad Francis Chávez, to my abuelo, Luis Alfonso Avilés.

CONTENTS

Acknowledgments   1

Introduction   2

one   6

Beautiful Scars   7

Soul Mate   8

Beauty Sleep   9

Skin Of Your Tears   10

Sleeping Through The Smoke   11

The Frida In Her/The Diego In Me   13

Missing Your Touch   14

A Kiss   15

two   16

Polysyndeton Riot   17

Some Days   18

The Deep End   20

Chiaroscuro   21

Blues For Miles   22

Moksha   23

Telling The Bees   24

Writer's Block   25

three	26
Our Lament	28
Laid To Rest	29
Eloy, The Lion	30
Luisita, My Greñuda	32
Besa	34
My Daughter's Love	36
four	37
I Saw A Homeless Man Fall	38
The Moon	39
Tonic	40
Cafecito	41
Stratum	43
Chaos	44
Lately,	45
Donor	46
Scent	47
Shojo	48
Hydraulic Eyes	49

five   50

Fall In Love On Days   51

Insomniac's Note   52

Walking Between Raindrops   53

Lluvia   54

Desolación   55

Missing Verses   56

Falling Star   57

Ghosts   59

Her Dreams Are Normal   60

End of Conversation   61

[Exit Stage Left]   62

About The Author   63

More Books From El Zarape Press   64

Thank You, Readers   66

ACKNOWLEDGMENTS

To Daniel García Ordaz at El Zarape Press, thank you for knowing *Insomnia* had a brother not too far behind. Thank you for embracing this new project with dedication and trust.

Grateful acknowledgement to my friends in the poetry community for your friendship and support over the years, especially to Beat scholar Dr. Robert Earl Johnson Jr., Dr. David Bowles, and César De León for your helpful feedback on this project.

INTRODUCTION

Beatific: The Poems Of Edward Vidaurre

"Beat" means The Beatitudes of The Sermon on the Mount, found in the first book of the New Testament, and composed in contrast to the judgments of Old Testament Ten Commandments.

Blessed are the poor in spirit,
for theirs is the kingdom of heaven.
Blessed are they who mourn,
for they shall be comforted.
Blessed are the meek,
for they shall inherit the earth.
Blessed are they who hunger and thirst for righteousness,
for they shall be satisfied.
Blessed are the merciful,
for they shall obtain mercy.
Blessed are the pure of heart,
for they shall see God.
Blessed are the peacemakers,
for they shall be called children of God.
Blessed are they who are persecuted for the sake of righteousness,
for theirs is the kingdom of heaven.

Kerouac was sneered at during his lifetime when he insisted this was the secret meaning of the term Beat, but in retrospect we can see what a fine rubric for poetry he left behind. Beatific poetry. Poetry about the sleepless, the homeless, the hungry, the lovelorn, the sick, the persecuted innocents, the luckless, the poor ("pauvre," Kerouac told a French interviewer who asked him to define "beat"), the insane, the jilted, the abandoned, the divorced—in short, everything that everyone who is human (used as an adjective, not a noun) has ever been or ever will be. And because of this, not in spite of it, we are to inherit the Kingdom of Heaven, promises the sermon. Beat, but not beat down, Kerouac would say.

The poet who attempts to write such beatific poems has to have a pure heart, meaning he knows his heart is not pure, but his intentions are pure. Anything less than pure honesty jolts the reader. Edward Vidaurre's confessional poems in this collection honestly don't stray in this respect. You are listening to him like friend would over beers on front porch bench late at night, air humid with sorrow, but never with unredeemable sadness or judgment (those Ten Commandments).

The method here is fragmentation. Bits of dreams recorded at waking. Stanzas from lost and forgotten poems come to light as detritus shifts. Random knowledge appearing on Wikipedia-ed computer screen reads like personal prophecy. Glimpses rather than vistas. Fragments. In modern art, the still life has long been replaced by the collage. This is the way the mind works, certainly the suffering sleep-deprived mind, and Vidaurre's recording of it results in telepathic communication with reader, for reader's brain cannot fail to recognize its suffering twin (what Ginsberg said about the technique of Kerouac's novels). Such poems can only be written, as Vidaurre's poems are, in language with no dusty coating, not written because read elsewhere, instead always sincere. (I won't spoil the reader's forthcoming pleasure with quotations.)

Vidaurre's Los Angeles of these poems is the land of the dead that comes back to life every day, like the homeless man in one of these poems who only appears dead. This is why we miss LA when we leave it: we want to know what will happen next. Kerouac said LA was the "beatest" of all American cities, but he only intuited this, never lived there only passed through. Vidaurre's mother in 1992 LA tells him to run over rioters if they come to attack his car as he drives home to East Los after waiting tables in a Beverly Hills restaurant. LA is mother, father, stepfather, and prayers for the father to love the stepfather and the mother to forgive.

These LA family poems seem like precognitions of the speaker's elegiac view of his present—separations, love disappeared, impossible reconciliations, a child's belief in the magical ability to make things whole again. But the suffering in these lines is not unbearable in fact because it is bared, and there is, after all, that promised Kingdom of Heaven, and the poor of heart are still blessed, whether that Kingdom exists are not.

In its Buddhist shape, Beat poetry "accepts all loss forever." Which makes for inhuman poetry that belies our actual sufferings in life. *Beautiful Scars* is suffering as art, not art that denies suffering. Still beautiful. Beatific.

Rob Johnson
Starbucks at Fern, McAllen, Texas
April 12, 2015, 3—4 p.m.

Robert Earl Johnson Jr. is the author of *The Lost Years of William S. Burroughs: Beats in South Texas* and is the co-editor of *"The Beatest State in the Union": Texas and the Beat Generation of Writers.* Forthcoming is *Did Beatniks Kill John F. Kennedy? Bongo Joe's Requiem for the President.* Dr. Johnson teaches courses on south Texas literature and the "Beat" generation of writers at the University of Texas Rio Grande Valley. He is married to the poet Erika Garza Johnson, and they have two children, Cactus and Isabel.

Beautiful Scars

one.

"When wounds are healed by love,

The scars are beautiful."

~David Bowles, *Shattering & Bricolage*

Edward Vidaurre

Beautiful Scars

When we met, she worried about the scars. Asked that I
close my eyes forever if I wanted to love her for just as long .
. . deep beautiful scars that pierced through her like a
falsetto. White lines that resembled rivers across the sky —
contrails. Years of anguish broke the surface of her skin.
When I arrived, I thought I could heal them . . . I thought I
was the one to mend, be a salve. The scars are now on me.
Now it's her turn to close her eyes forever . . . give me a shot
at this thing called love.

Soul Mate

You are my love story.
Without looking, there you were. You entered my heart
through the brush of your lips on mine, through each
detailed fingertip caress, through the aura of scented
orgasms. We didn't meet. There we were — in each other — all
along.

Edward Vidaurre

Beauty Sleep

This insomnia drinks coffee. I know it does.

It unravels dreams that follow

    the pheromones of virgin mermaids.

The cat lady is hissing

    into the night, in search

    of the calico kitten with hazel orbs.

You lay in bed, like a queen,

    beautiful like the fists of a heavyweight champion . . .

    dreaming of a romantic dinner

    on gold-leaf fine china plates.

I watch your breath seep

    from your mouth and jump off

    your lips . . .

    your breasts heave.

Skin of Your Tears
(After José José's "Almohada")

I've been sifting through the dead skin you left behind on your pillow for the past two nights. Your scent is all but gone. A lone hair tangles itself on my fingers. The tear stains never dried. I will lay here with a view of a street that saw you drive off to the south as my prayers took off into the unforgiving night. I heard your voice cry out. Got up to look. . . . nothing there but a pair of mismatched stiletto heels, one with a torn strap, the other with a scuff mark. I turned off the lights about three minutes past one in the morning. . . . Next to me, your scent returned to reclaim its layer of skin that fell off your shadow, leaving me alone with your tears that take up your side of the bed.

Edward Vidaurre

Sleeping Through the Smoke

I read some Rumi before bed and in the dream I was on my way to a Bed & Breakfast but never left town due to some odd circumstance. I smoked several cigarettes in my dream as I sat on the ledge of a high-rise apartment complex. As I got up, I walked down the open-air staircase. I passed indigenous families talking in their native Nawat. I understood them but could not answer back. They would just say, "He's the poet who almost jumped. It seems he loves her still."

*Pipil (Nawat in the native tongue) is an ancient language spoken in Central America, similar to the ancient Aztec Náhuatl.

Beautiful Scars

Edward Vidaurre

The Frida In Her/The Diego In Me

So we fought and left the Wal-Mart shopping cart full of groceries and a box of *adult chewing gum* under the French bread and apples. We drove back to your apartment, just south on Sugar Road, where they caught the flasher that was terrorizing university students—all girls. There, I refused to take off my socks because my little toe was afraid of touching the ground and looked funny. We started over. We kissed and laughed at the silliness of our first fight. We kissed some more and decided to order a pizza. I was not a smoker back then, but I sure could've used one later that night.

Missing Your Touch

Blue walls

Laid back night

Under the super moon

Everything glowed

Beautiful sounds

Always

Leave me

Looking for

Something to decipher

A Kiss

It has to be triumphant. It's too personal. It's cosmic. It's dangerous. It's specific. It's got to be original each time. It can be funny, serious, or delicious, but never just a kiss for the sake of a kiss. The best kisses are when no words can be exchanged afterwards because you're too busy catching your breath or gathering yourself from the explosion.

"Some things remain fragments — just the lyrics and melodies or a line or two or a verse."

~Tracy Chapman

two.

Polysyndeton Riot

I remember my mom telling me to run over anyone who got in my way during the L.A. Riots as I made my way through South Central to pick her up from work. My 1970 Buick Skylark had a full tank of gas. I prayed the sniper's stray bullet wouldn't hit my gas tank. I was ready to flatten bodies, and it was in April of 1992, and I was nineteen, and I was scared, and I didn't loot, and I played Ice Cube, and they did "Burn That Motherfucker Down!"

Some Days

not even music does it. Chocolate ice cream doesn't do it. She sits looking at old photographs in silence. The kind of place that does it serves hot tea instead of coffee. I love coffee. Hold the pen knowing the blank page is perfect. Days play out. My favorite chair is uncomfortable. I move. The rain is perfect; she sleeps through it. Its loudness cripples me; meanwhile she looks for that pill fix. Bliss is in catching the last fly in the room after we've destroyed the air around us. It's never too late to begin a life of love. The dancing hula girl on her dashboard: I want to stop it. The lone penny left on the hot asphalt outside a gas station: I want to pick it up. The marker with a missing top causing it to go dry: I want to cover it because it just makes things better. Is it a better world? Maybe so. Then we hear of 150 people being vaporized on the side of a mountain and we feel like shit. That's when I set my alarm and count sheep — count them one by bloody one. Some days, not even music does it. Even my shadow walks faster than me.

Edward Vidaurre

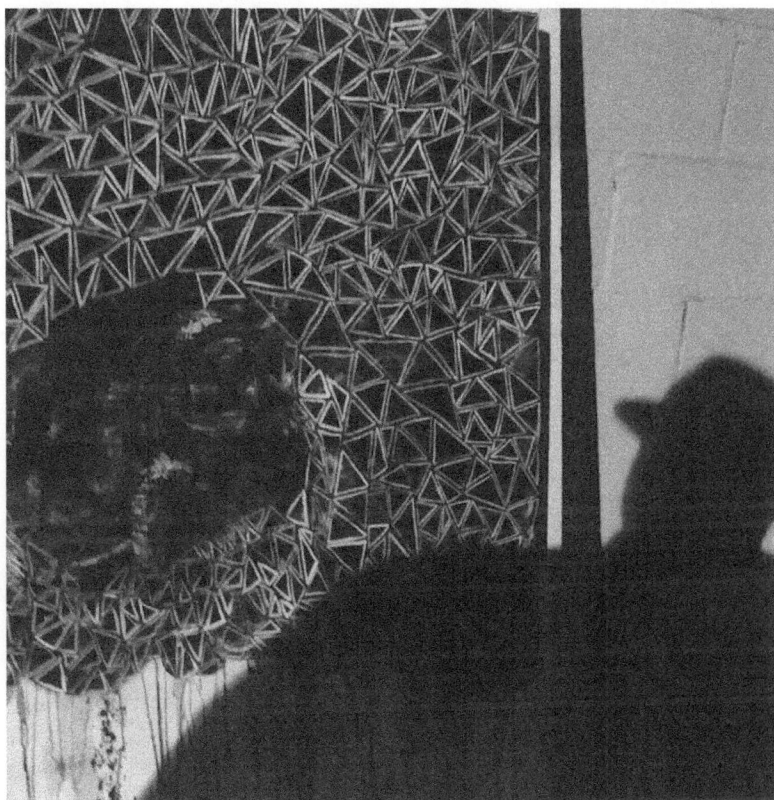

The Deep End

Mermaids drink from my veins. They search for sea salt.

Amar, respirar, cantar, criar niños con voces poéticas.

Retire to Antioch, sell whispered elegies from a food truck.

Edward Vidaurre

Chiaroscuro

Somewhere between the shadows that walk during our sleep paralysis, there's a song. It has no color, veiled like a procession of widows on their way to visit their handsome dead. It strums and strings along, never giving itself in absolution to sorrow . . . instead walking, and singing a new song of hope – a bright tune.

Blues For Miles

"It Never Entered My Mind" smoothly makes its way to my ears from the speakers in the corner. The tune is so beautiful—feels like I'm at a piano bar in a big city. . . . I can almost sense the doors opening and men and women huddling inside to avoid the rain outside, laughing as they hold their fingers up to announce the number of people in their party.

Outside though, it's humid. Inside I'm drinking soup to feed this minor cold, families here eat and speak loudly over Miles Davis. . . . If they only knew—if they just listened for a bit—maybe they too would smell the petrichor every time the door opened, and let Miles do the rest. . . .

Edward Vidaurre

Moksha*
(mo ·ksha / ˈmōkSHə/)

A wanderer takes to the air, waltzing in a cloud,
peeling though the skin of the passing haze —
otherworldly —
a spirit rising,
dropping embers of himself, effervescing into the mouths of
the moribund
on his transcendence —
away from purgatory towns of deaf mice
bypassing weary *curanderas,*
barefoot children of the *colonias,*
a decrepit hospice with the elders of Old Testament lore,
becoming a buoyant mystic blowing the final horn,
knocking on Nirvana's gates,
releasing his song

*In Indian philosophies and religions: *freedom from the
differentiated, temporal, and mortal world of ordinary experience;
liberation from the cycle of death and rebirth; from Sanskrit*

Telling The Bees

I'll knock on the beehive that hangs outside your house, near the tree that hides stories of a noose that silenced every leaf this summer. I'm telling the bees. I'm telling them about the day comedy committed suicide and every depressed person walked the streets in procession, pouring their sadness into the gutters that also washed away the dark crimson from Eric Garner's neck, from Emmett Till's eyes, from Octavio Rojas Hernandez's journals, from my dad's vomit into the eyes of cancer.

I'm telling the bees of your departure into the arms of the trumpet's wail, of your heart's mischief with the decorated hero's tainted star, and the riffs of the cover band's mute guitar strings.

I'm telling the bees. I'm whispering. I'm singing it to them. I'm telling them . . . interrupting them, as they sting me one by one. I'll make them listen to me.

I'm telling the bees. I'm telling the bees, gently, but I'm telling them . . . that when you return, just walk right in. I'll be producing honey in the back porch. I'll be making it sweet — producing a fresh batch of . . .

Welcome home, My Love.

Editor's note: The **telling of the bees** is a traditional Celtic and European custom, borrowed from the ancient Egyptians and later the ancient Greeks, who revered honeybees as messengers to the gods. Beekeepers in Scotland and England, for example, tell the bees of the death of a beekeeper, as well as important events in their keeper's lives, such as births, marriages, or departures and returns in the household. The bees were most commonly told of deaths in their master's family." (From Wikipedia, the free encyclopedia and beegood.co.uk)

Edward Vidaurre

Writer's Block

Everyone is writing good poetry tonight.

Everyone, but me.

"Don't grieve. Anything you lose comes around in another form."

~Rumi

three.

Our Lament

dad.
tears.
dad. more. tears.
dad.
love.

Edward Vidaurre

Laid to Rest

He never owned a dog, my father. No one can claim territory to his grave. . . . Moctezuma II wouldn't allow it. I promise to cover his body with peach and avocado skins. His face will be washed with pomegranate drops from refugee children's fingertips. . . . I'll let his *cotorro* fly north, never to return. The priest will cover us all with incense and Holy Water and pray.

Eloy, The Lion

I.

. . . and when I get the news of your passing, the sun will emerge with liver spots that will cast shades on the earth. People will fight for the parking spots where there is no shine because leather seats after hours in the sun . . . well, burn. Your shadow will walk away into the fragments of the morning fog. The moon will understand. I've told her about you many times. She will weep into the ocean and curse the highest mountain with darkness. Church bells will ring and incense will burn for you. I will think too much about it and dig up every worm in my backyard and chew on it. I will want to know everything about you, a bit late. You never knew much about my poetry, but it's okay because now you're my new poetry. I will keep you alive and your hair will continue to grow. I'm glad you had a ridiculously handsome laugh. Even when you tried being mean, you were tender on the eyes.

Take the color blue with you, like the uniforms of many years of hard work. Take with you all the gold, like the ring with the peridot stone. Take the color yellow as well and hand it to my biological father and tell him not to be jealous, but thankful. Maybe you can sneak a lock of Mother's hair into heaven, put it at the feet of Mary, and walk away in silence. She will know. Take 10 degrees of heat and toss it into St. Jude's garden. This cancer thing, leave it behind: let us figure it out. Look into the mirror before you go. Stand up straight and see my face on the reflection, the face of your three beautiful girls and two other boys, your grandchildren too. You did good, Pop. Feel the breath of your wife on your face and her soft hands in yours.

II.

My daughter asked, "Is he my last grandpa?" . . . I said "Yes."

She cried.
    I cried.
        I explained.
            She understood.

She ran off to draw and color a picture in pinks, blues and yellows
with ribbons and tears. I told her to draw an avocado.

She asked after the drawing was complete, "What is going to happen to him?"

I told her, "He will become a new season, a mix between spring and summer, a dash of winter and a chunk of fall."

III.

In heaven, he is on the radar: INCOMING:
"Eloy, the Lion!"

Luisita, My Greñuda

When she came home, jaundice was the first gold she wore. She sat up straight and laughed at the avocado that slipped from her feeble hands. When she fell off the bed, Jesus, Mary and Joseph simultaneously covered their ears. Remember when she ate her first fruit—a mango—and loved long baths? Now she talks of less baths and more cuddles, of more candy and less broccoli, of Lego worlds and doll clothing, of wanting a convertible and waiting for that next tooth to emerge, of school bullies and kindness.

Luisita: "Daddy, can you make sure in the second grade they start calling me by my first name?"
Me: Sure thing, Bella. Of course I will, my love.

Besa

for Bella

I will keep it 'til the last breath
of your favorite star, bird, poem, and color

> Your presence warms my
> heart. Your hazel eyes
> see through my wretched
> and surprising days of mirth

Your voice is so tiny
but peregrinates to every
corner of my world —
washing away every tincture of torment

> My *besa* for you is worth
> more than a thousand kites

For you are my love
You are my faith.
You are my treasure.
You are my laughter.

> —my oral law
> —my evolution
> —my only necessity

*Besa in Albanian Muslim culture means keeping one's faith, one's
promise, one's word of honor.*

Edward Vidaurre

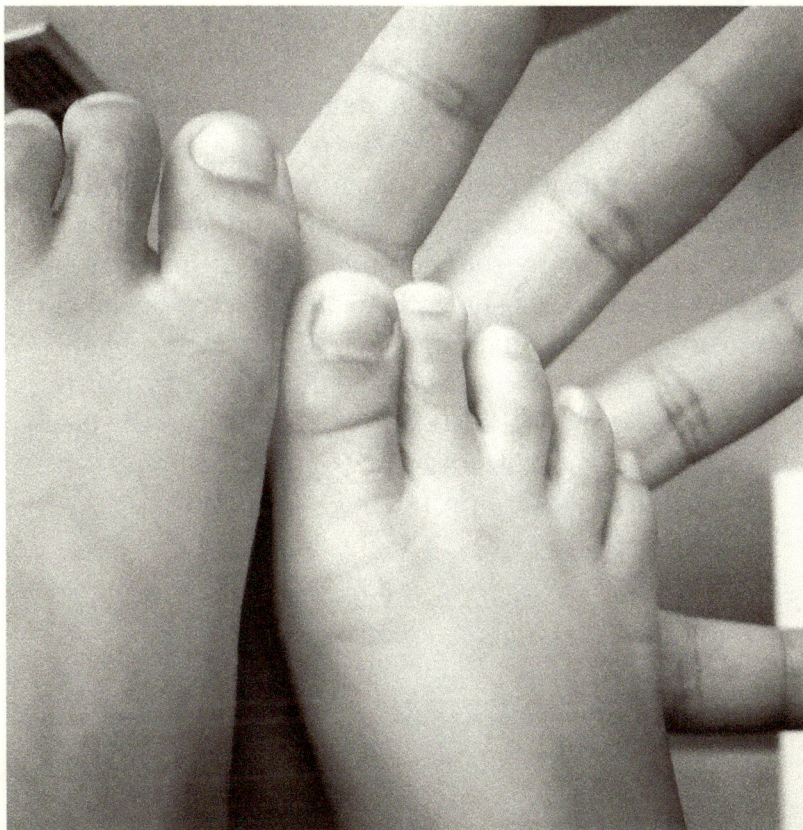

My Daughter's Love

She feels it's her duty to wipe tears from her father's eyes.
She cries with me, tear for tear. She makes sure extra ones
come out of her hazel eyes to match my grief. Her full lips
fold the tears that trickle down her face and she drinks the
sea that falls from my soul and tucks it in a corner in the
back of her heart where she gathers all the sorrow. She nods
her head as I speak, making sure I understand that she
understands. She is six, so I change the subject by putting
sorrow in my back pocket to take out later when the black
night turns a deep purple and eats away at the hours where
no shadows are prohibited — until morn.

four.

"Love all, trust a few, do wrong to none."

~William Shakespeare, *All's Well That Ends Well*

I Saw A Homeless Man Fall

face first into a busy street. I remember it because the air had the stench of urine and my mom told me to make sure the car door remained locked. The concrete drank the blood through its cracks. Another man bent down to check his pockets for cash or maybe a bottle and kicked him in the ribs when he came up empty. No one helped. He laid there motionless. I want to imagine he was helped after we drove off as the light turned green. But I dreamt that he was not. He still lays in the gutter of my dreams, in pain. I want to think of him as a poet. Writing sonnets and prose. I want to think of him pushing a cart filled with manuscripts and surviving on hot soup. I imagine him raising pigeons that coo his stanzas to the beat of tin drums and scraped washboards. Sitting around a fire blazing and sending embers to the heavens with new psalms for a new book . . . a new testament. His name is hope. He brushes off the hunger. He sings and angels listen. We pass by—the light turns green—he is standing upright.

Edward Vidaurre

The Moon

is the most beautiful I've seen since I stopped taking her for
granted. People are coming out of taverns and apartment
complexes, two-story homes and trailer parks to see. They're
pulling over to gawk at her in the total darkness of the
Petrified Forest on Route 66. But she belongs to me tonight,
and I will not share her. She showed me her nakedness at
noon, while others were being too busy to notice. She's
slimmer than usual in her fullness. I noticed. She's reading
my poems on her reflection in the sea.

Tonic

The green wind slices through the darkest part of my dreams. I wish I could catch every breath you take in your sleep tonight. It is nights like this that words in my head out-dual any song. Hungry cats cry for me. I want to be your venom, not your antidote. I want to be the lyrics that spill from your mouth as you slumber. I want to be what keeps you smashed— your gin.

Cafecito

You injure when
in heat. You caress my tongue,
and my vernacular doesn't jive in
the barrio when I sip you.
You make *chismes* about *aquellos*
that much more interesting.
I pull you in—
a straight shot.
Cafecito, soy adicto.
Cafecito por la mañana,
Cafecito por la tarde,
sangre de insomnia,
negra hermosa,
amarga, y ardiente:
Life-blood.

Edward Vidaurre

Stratum

When there is no longer room for sanity, I finally fall asleep, and dreams take over. In the dream, a woman walks slowly, wearing a long gown and a *rebozo* over her head, covering her face. She knocks on every door she passes. No one answers. She turns around, and I am standing in front of her. There's a sweeping silence. In the air, the smell of knives slices through our breathing. On her face, a beak and a forked tongue. In her hands: a cracked rib. I open my mouth—she feeds me snails and salt. We fight through the foam of ecstasy. Spitting iridescent *caracoles* into her womb in hopes of waking up to a new delusion.

Chaos

(after Gigi Morales, *Chaos in love*, 2012, acrylic on canvas 5′
x 4′)

Her mouth
d
r
o
p
s

vacant lyrics into
an empty glass

perhaps
it's a howl

perhaps
it's an echo

perhaps
it's a murmur

Lately,

love tastes like broken English, feels like jive talk, sounds like the water that sloshes under the pier as you look over the *madera* at a close distance to the cotton candy. It feels like a cat searching for a warm engine in the winter. *Amor ahogado, sin ganas,* distracted, over-dosing on false hope and kind words from poets that hide behind sonnets and suede shoes. Lately, love is *like,* and *like* is not enough. Love needs *suero,* a drip bag of *aguántate un poco mas.* But I'll wait for a transplant—wait for a donor. And somewhere out there, soon, someone will die of heartache and maybe, just maybe, the donor and I will be a match.

Donor

The way she took her coffee: black.

She drank the bitter java and kept a smile, as if thinking,
"I hate coffee! But for you — anything!"
I loved her for it.

I would give her my eyes that morning as a gift.
She walked away, hazel orbs in hand.
I waited until she turned the corner —
That's when her scent left me.

I walked into oncoming traffic.
Parts for everyone.

Edward Vidaurre

Scent

I will etch out love notes on brick and post
In the dirty alleys of New Orleans on Fat Tuesday,
inscribe on ancient papyrus.
When the ink runs out, I will cut a finger
or two, fill in the blank spaces, completing
the last stanza of a Beat poem
telling you I've got it bad for you.

Shōjō*

(a drunken haiku)

Mayáhuel, take me
out of Tijuana dirt roads
into a shack,

                drunk

*Japanese deity — god of drunkenness

Edward Vidaurre

Hydraulic Eyes

Lowrider eyes
    weighed down by blue
Eye-shadow overlooking
    labios rellenos that confess
A night wrapped in satin—
    dreams like a cocoon
    waiting to unfurl
Her black   and   white wings

Beautiful Scars

"Let our scars fall in love."

~Andrew Boyd

five.

Edward Vidaurre

Fall In Love On Days

when the weather outside coincides with the season. When gas is less by the gallon than the week before. Fall in love when the milk in the fridge expires. When a Big Mac tastes like heaven. Fall in love on frigid days that allow for reading a mystery novel. Fall in love to the sound of a distant trumpet. When poems speak to you – or don't. Fall in love when you accept your fat. Fall in love when you have a month to live. Love on Mondays. Fall in love during the season finale. Love because hating hurts. Fall in love with her eyes, her lips, her voice, her off-key singing. Fall in love in the shower, up on the roof, behind the bleachers. Fall in love in November. Count her freckles. Erase her sadness. Fill her empty arms. Love her farts. Fall in love with her funny toe. Love her madly.

Insomniac's Note

I can't sleep. Because someone asked me what is love, and all I could think of was a tree filled with sleeping birds and wide-awake cats. And you . . . being away. Because when I think of love, I get up and walk to a window, any window, and I see you turn corners. It's cold outside and the wind bites at you every time. It's always cold, and you always fade into the quiet world. The air smells of onions. . . . I cry into my hands . . . then it starts to rain.

Edward Vidaurre

Walking Between Raindrops

your scent: petrichor

we will walk between raindrops
staying dry and lost

on the outside, wet and true
on the inside, you're peeling apart

Lluvia

Outside it rained —

    A desperate downpour

that caused   piano vibrations

on the dry   earth

with each   flit,   flit

Inside we clashed —

You suffered   through each sigh

I inhaled the scent

                              from your hair —

     a flash!

followed by   thunder!

Desolación

like her antepasados,
she covers her mirrors
during thunderstorms

relámpagos contra su reflexión

afuera — llueve
sin cesar

adentro se ahoga

Missing Verses

You are the only one between heaven and earth that matters.
I drank from the river that turned up missing verses:

> *I made love to her*
> *elbows, knees and toes.*
> *She wore a tangerine*
> *Bra that pushed her cleavage up*
> *to her chin.*
> *I made love to her chin too.*
> *She drank wine and giggled after*
> *every sip.*
> *made love to her throat and she*
> *danced around me.*
> *Like a hummingbird . . . I made*
> *love to her in mid-air.*

I turned into an owl for you —
To chase a falling star.

Falling Star

When a mother cries . . .
The weeds outgrow the grass
Cigarette butts collect on my patio floor
Ashes stick to my skin—my lungs turn blue
The legs of the barbecue pit become buried
The cat hunts and brings me headless grackles
A wild wind makes off with my fedora
A lone blue star from a child's glittery craft, long
completed, unglues, rends itself,
shows up unannounced at my feet
as I line up the yellow thread from my socks to my
toes
The batteries on my remote leak
The TV set goes mute
Lights dim as my beard begins to grow out of kilter
My skin gets ashy
The shed out back corrodes
Wicks from candles burn down, drowning in their
own wax
I write while crying in a dark corner
Until rocks turn to sand, and sand turns to dust

Edward Vidaurre

Ghosts

When we sleep, our faces are borrowed by ghosts, and we

are left with nothing but peelings of each other. My heavy

body struggles for position against your nightmares. I sleep

in the nude; my skin gives light to the purple night as it

molts on the sheets. The walls perspire and cry onto the

shaggy white carpet. We breathe and die a little. Sometimes

we wake up and don't recognize our own frowns. Maybe

our faces ended up in another town, on another couple —

naked dreamers — who will wake . . . finally recognizing

their own smiles.

Her Dreams Are Normal

It's a cold day.
My city feels wounded by
The light rain that falls.
On days like this,
She would ask me to open
A window. We would listen to
The pelting on the tin roof across our
Apartment. The light that came in showed
The bruises on her legs from where
Pleasure fell off its trapeze at two a.m.
We would fall asleep in each other's embrace,
Waking from an image of a child tugging at his mother's
breasts with baby soft lips, Waiting for the milk of life to fill
him.
       Her dreams are normal —
       A dog, a home, children.
I wake up, and look
around the room for
that child wearing scuffed cowboy boots,
playing with his sister's naked Barbie doll.

End of Conversation

We speak through beads of sweat, through dust particles that are prevalent just as the sun starts its descent into the thirsty ocean. We speak after six, again just before dinner — when the home smells of chicken broth, and just before the last of the cilantro sprigs's backstroke. We speak late, her hands tucked under the pillow. I speak with my hands caressing her back. My hands — the ones that memorized each curve and, like a blind man reading Braille, can read each of her scars with my eyes closed. Her mouth opens to speak, but the breaths — against my skin — are lacerations that say it all. We've said it best by saying nothing at all.

[Exit Stage Left]

[I'm imagining this room — a window by the tub. The sun is beaming through the white sequined curtains. She bathes in fruits: peach skins and grapes. Curtains jazz with the breeze. The walls of brick and post grin. She ignores the action of the room coming to life around her. She outlines her lips. He stands next to her refilling her glass with Chartreuse, and she fills his mouth with kisses as she hums tunes from a Lost Generation.]

About The Author

Edward Vidaurre is the 2018-2019 Poet Laureate of McAllen, Texas. Vidaurre is a voice in Latino literature and Beat poetry. His work appears in numerous anthologies and journals, including *The Beatest State in the Union: An Anthology of Beat Texas Writers and in Poetry Of Resistance, Arriba Baseball!, Juventud!* and *Boundless — the Anthology of the Valley International Poetry Festival*, and in literary journals, such as *La Bloga's On Line Floricanto, Bordersenses, RiversEdge, Interstice, La Noria Literary Journal, Harbinger Asylum, Left Hand of the Father, and Brooklyn & Boyle* — a newspaper published in East Los Angeles, his hometown.

His first collection of poetry, *I Took My Barrio On A Road Trip*, was published in 2013 and his second collection, *Insomnia* (El Zarape Press), was published in 2014.

Conceived in El Salvador and born in Los Angeles, California, in 1973, Vidaurre is the founder of Pasta, Poetry, and Vino. His work has been nominated for the Pushcart Prize. He resides in the Rio Grande Valley.

He has been listed in *Letras Latinas List of 2013* A Year In Poetry: a Weblog of the literary program of the Institute for Latino Studies, University of Notre Dame as well as *La Bloga's On Line Floricanto Best Poems of 2013* (list of six poets).

Vidaurre co-edited *TWENTY: Poems in Memoriam*, an anthology in response to the Newtown, CT, tragedy.

MORE BOOKS FROM EL ZARAPE PRESS

Insomnia by **Edward Vidaurre**

poems inspired by insomnia and the vivid dream-like
imagery that a lack of sleep creates
ISBN-10: 1499525796

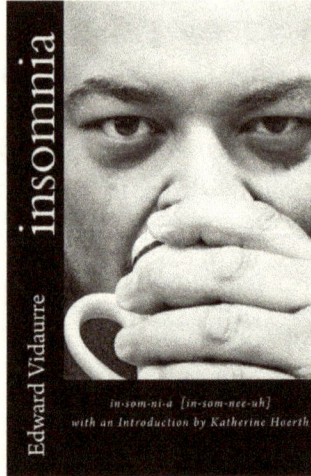

*You Know What I'm Sayin'? (Poetry*Drama)*
by **Daniel García Ordaz**

a celebration of the common experience of language and
culture
ISBN-10: 0978995414

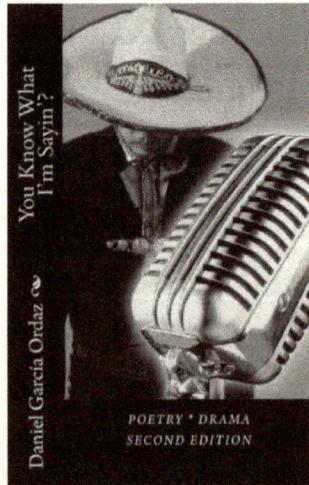

Edward Vidaurre

Twenty: In Memoriam (by several poets from across the U.S.)

in response to the school shootings at Sandy Hook Elem., in Newtown, CT, on 12/14/ 2012
ISBN-10: 1494326752

Boundless: The Anthology of the Rio Grande Valley Int'l. Poetry Festival

Published annually by El Zarape Press, proud sponsor of V.I.P.F.

www.valleypoetryfest.org

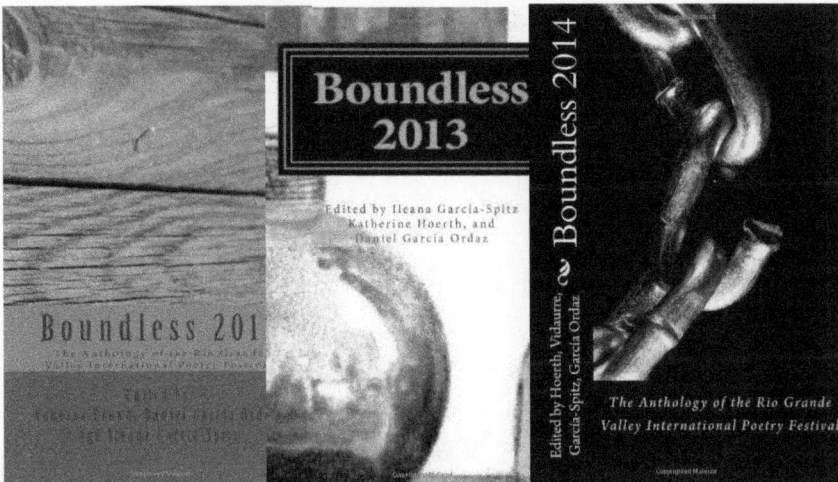

Dear Reader!

Thank you for reading my collection of poetry! Now that you've finished my latest offering to the poetry gods, I'd love to get your feedback through an honest review at amazon.com and goodreads.com as well as any other literary site you visit. Video reviews would be cool too!

Please let me know about YOUR #BeautifulScars at our new Page on Facebook: https://www.facebook.com/BeautifulScarsElegiacBeatPoems.

Please follow me on twitter, Instagram and/or Facebook and let me know when your review is posted. I'm available for workshops, literary events, and school visits via Skype or in person.

Once again, many thanks for reading *Beautiful Scars: Elegiac Beat Poems* and — if you read *Insomnia*, or my earlier work, *I Took My Barrio On A Road Trip*, kudos to you!

Sincerely,

Edward Vidaurre
#BeautifulScars

www.ingramcontent.com/pod-product-compliance
Lightning Source LLC
Chambersburg PA
CBHW020951030426
42339CB00004B/46